AFRICAN BLOOD
CVO
covert vampiric operations

D1203227

IDW Publishing • San Diego

script by **El Torres**

pencils & inks by **Luis Czerniawski**

color by **Fran Gamboa**

lettering by **JC Ruiz**
Sulaco Studios

editing by **Kris Oprisko**

collection edits by **Dene Nee**

IDW Publishing is
Ted Adams, President
Robbie Robbins, EVP/Sr. Graphic Artist
Chris Ryall, Publisher/Editor-in-Chief
Clifford Meth, EVP of Strategies/Editorial
Alan Payne, VP of Sales
Marci Kahn, Executive Assistant
Neil Uyetake, Art Director
Tom Waltz, Editor
Andrew Steven Harris, Editor
Chris Mowry, Graphic Artist
Amauri Osorio, Graphic Artist
Dene Nee, Graphic Artist/Editor
Matthew Ruzicka, CPA, Controller
Alonzo Simon, Shipping Manager
Kris Oprisko, Editor/Foreign Lic. Rep

www.idwpublishing.com
ISBN: 978-1-60010-210-3

11 10 09 08   1 2 3 4 5

Special thanks to Cristina Urdiales and James Heffron for their help and kind assistance.

KONAMI

Table of Contents

Chapter 1

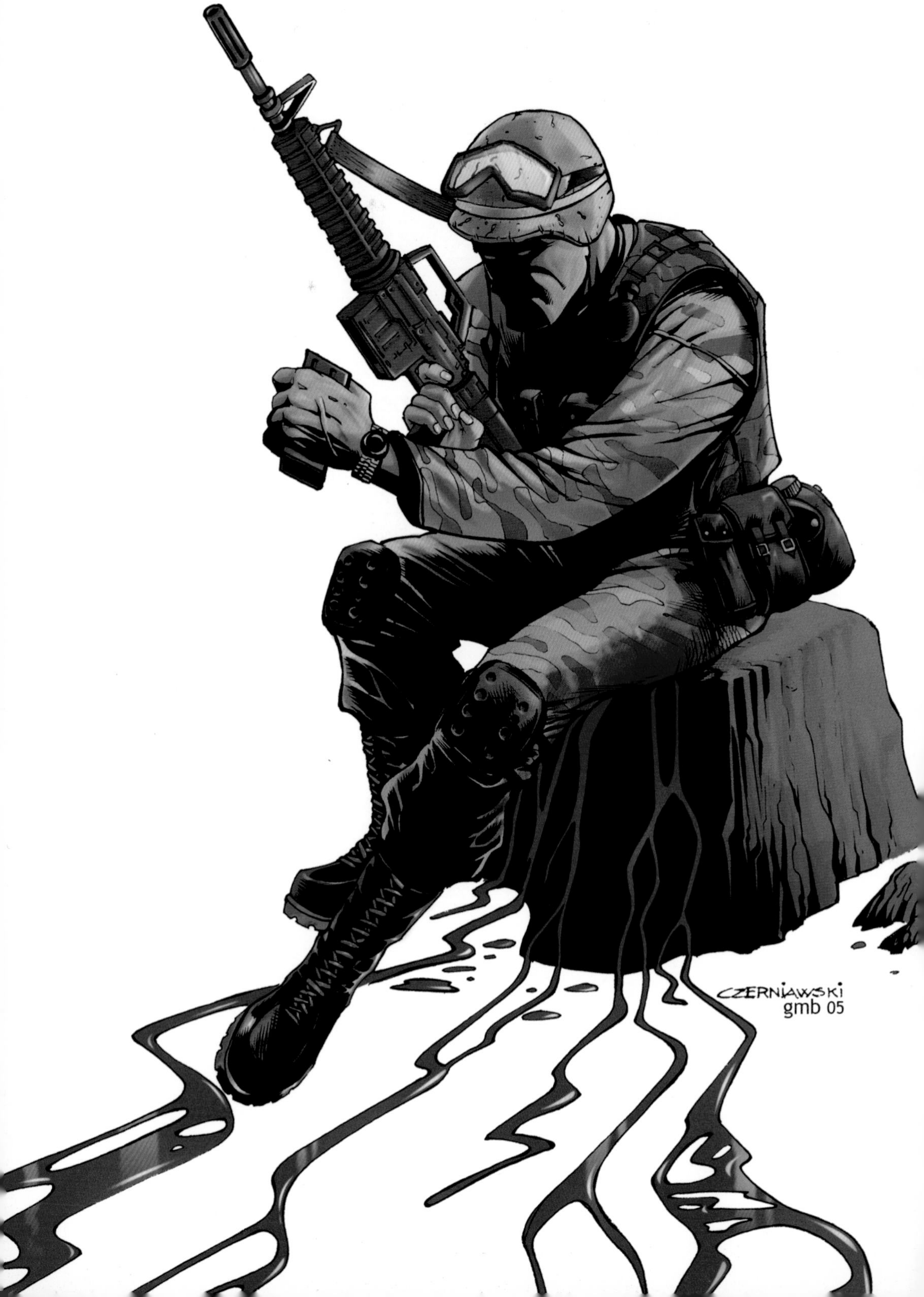

CZERNIAWSKI
gmb 05

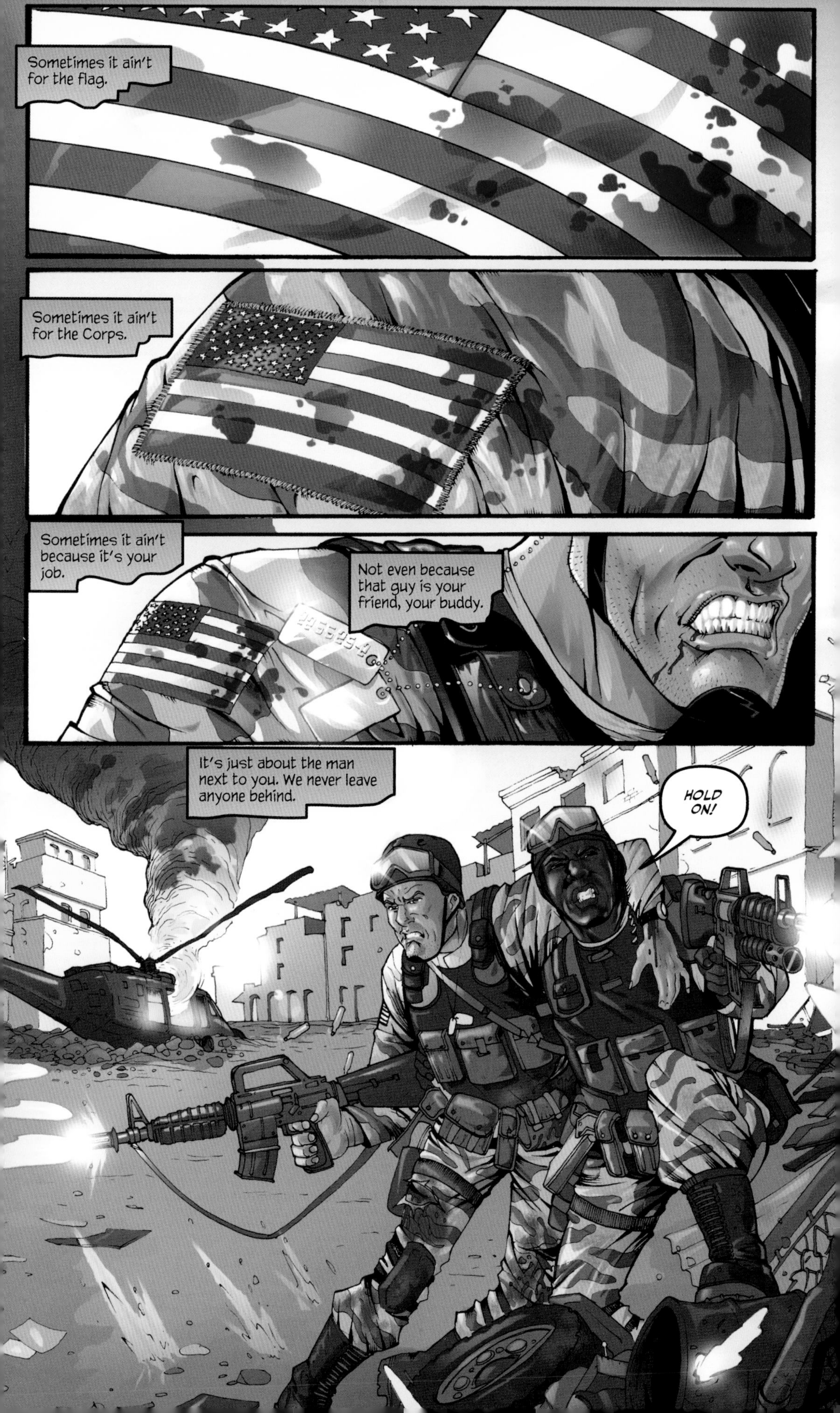
Sometimes it ain't for the flag.
Sometimes it ain't for the Corps.
Sometimes it ain't because it's your job.
Not even because that guy is your friend, your buddy.
It's just about the man next to you. We never leave anyone behind.
HOLD ON!

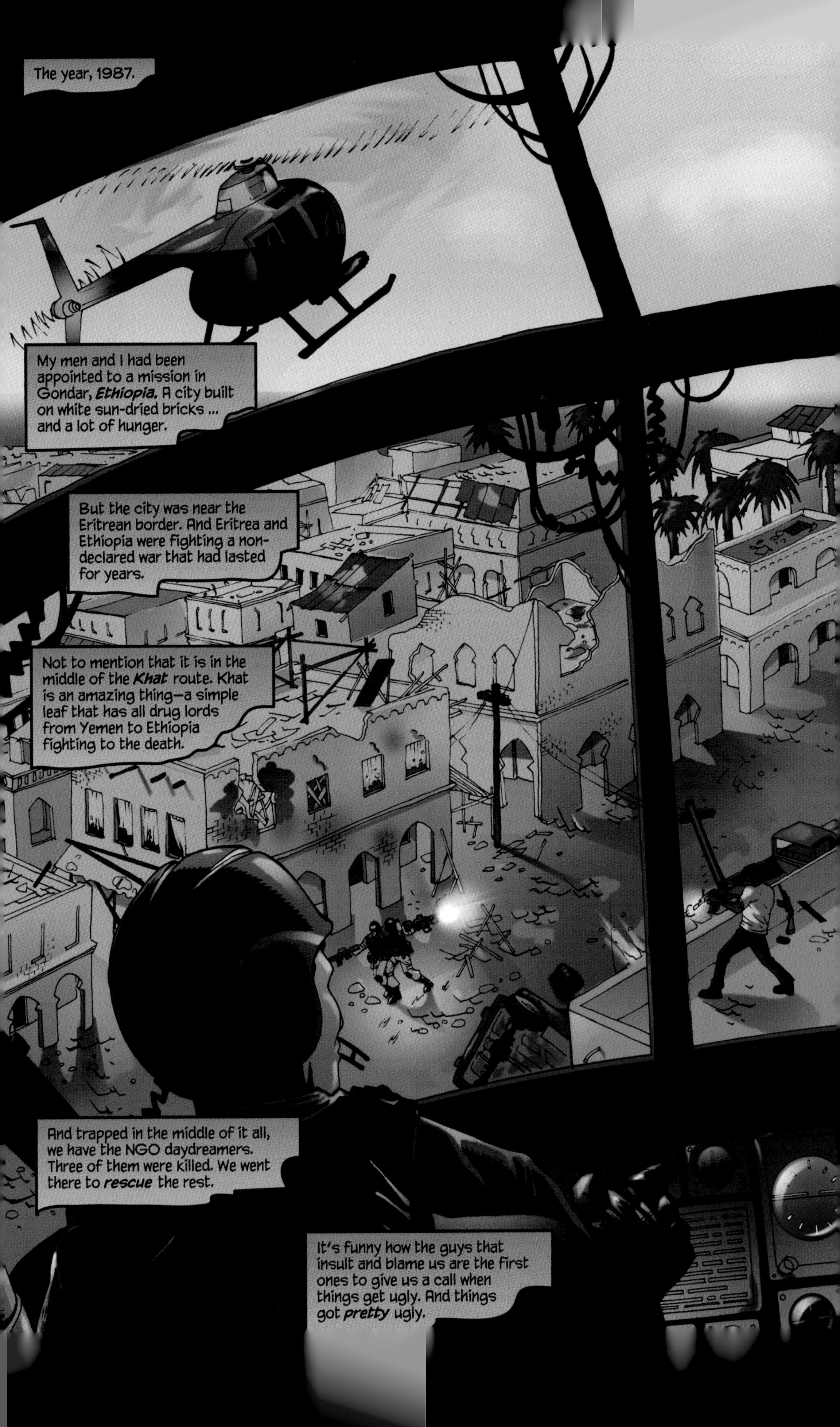
The year, 1987.
My men and I had been appointed to a mission in Gondar, *Ethiopia.* A city built on white sun-dried bricks ... and a lot of hunger.
But the city was near the Eritrean border. And Eritrea and Ethiopia were fighting a non-declared war that had lasted for years.
Not to mention that it is in the middle of the *Khat* route. Khat is an amazing thing—a simple leaf that has all drug lords from Yemen to Ethiopia fighting to the death.
And trapped in the middle of it all, we have the NGO daydreamers. Three of them were killed. We went there to *rescue* the rest.
It's funny how the guys that insult and blame us are the first ones to give us a call when things get ugly. And things got *pretty* ugly.

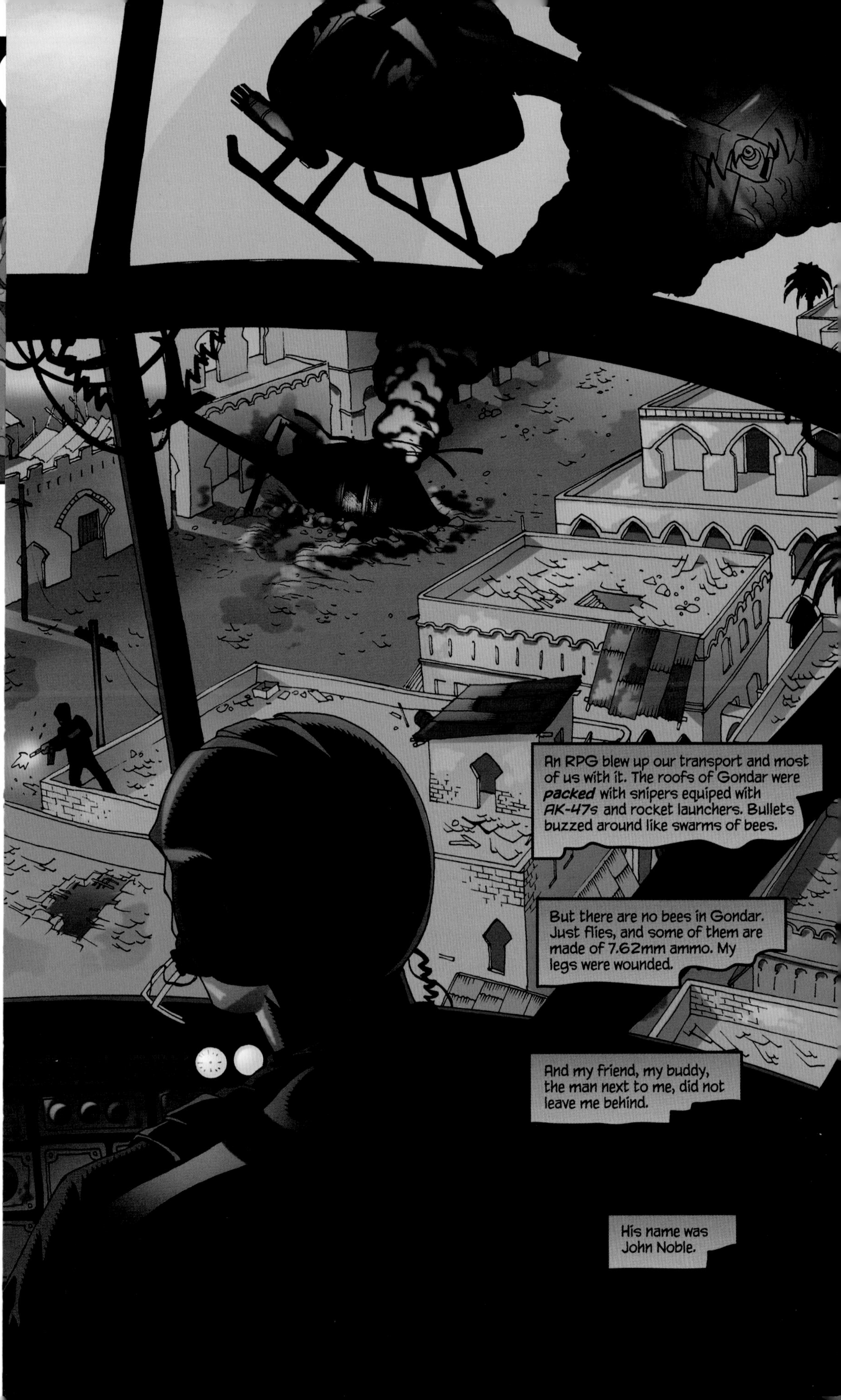
An RPG blew up our transport and most of us with it. The roofs of Gondar were *packed* with snipers equiped with *AK-47s* and rocket launchers. Bullets buzzed around like swarms of bees.
But there are no bees in Gondar. Just flies, and some of them are made of 7.62mm ammo. My legs were wounded.
And my friend, my buddy, the man next to me, did not leave me behind.
His name was John Noble.

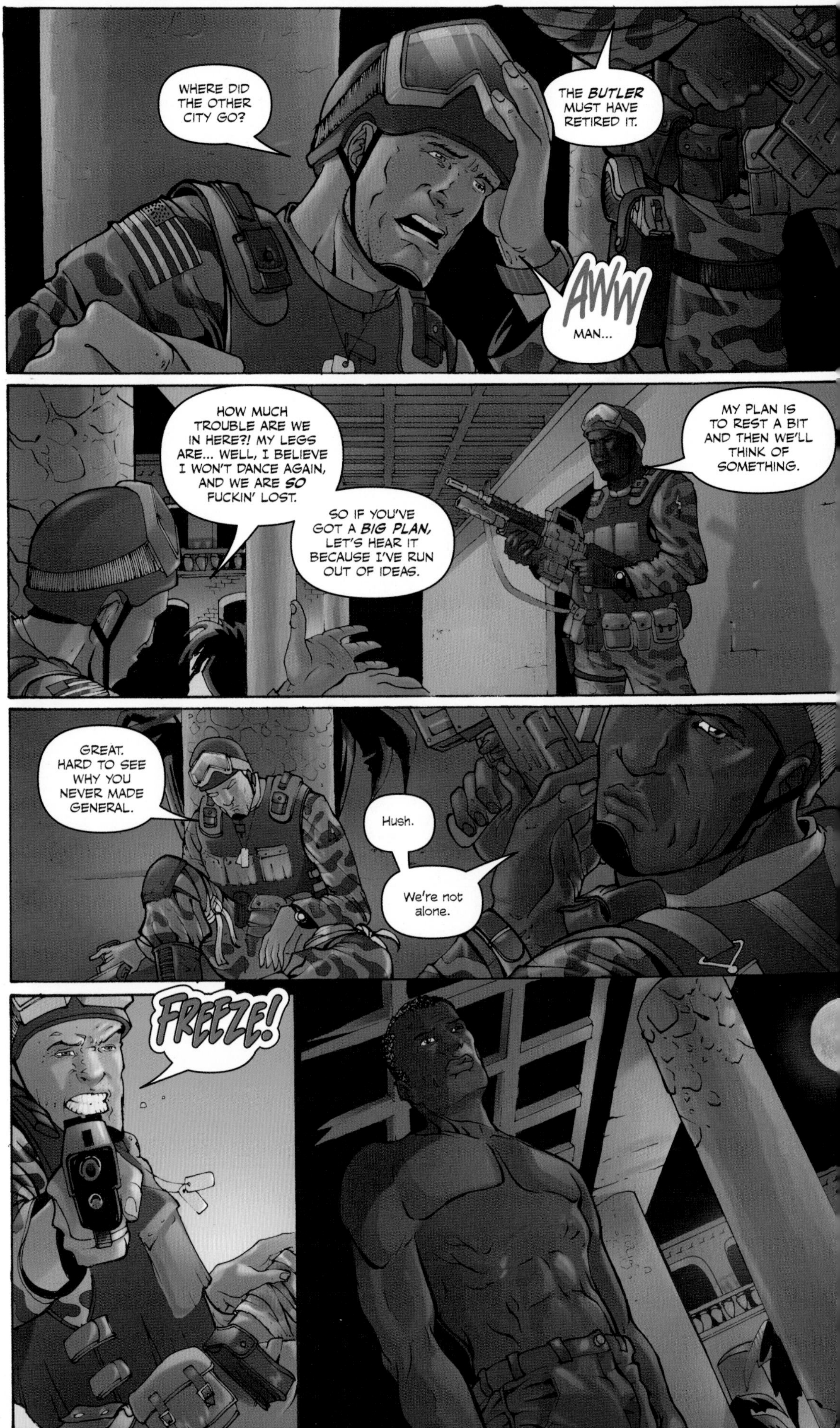
WHERE DID THE OTHER CITY GO?
THE BUTLER MUST HAVE RETIRED IT.
AWW
MAN...
HOW MUCH TROUBLE ARE WE IN HERE?! MY LEGS ARE... WELL, I BELIEVE I WON'T DANCE AGAIN, AND WE ARE SO FUCKIN' LOST.
SO IF YOU'VE GOT A BIG PLAN, LET'S HEAR IT BECAUSE I'VE RUN OUT OF IDEAS.
MY PLAN IS TO REST A BIT AND THEN WE'LL THINK OF SOMETHING.
GREAT. HARD TO SEE WHY YOU NEVER MADE GENERAL.
Hush.
We're not alone.
FREEZE!

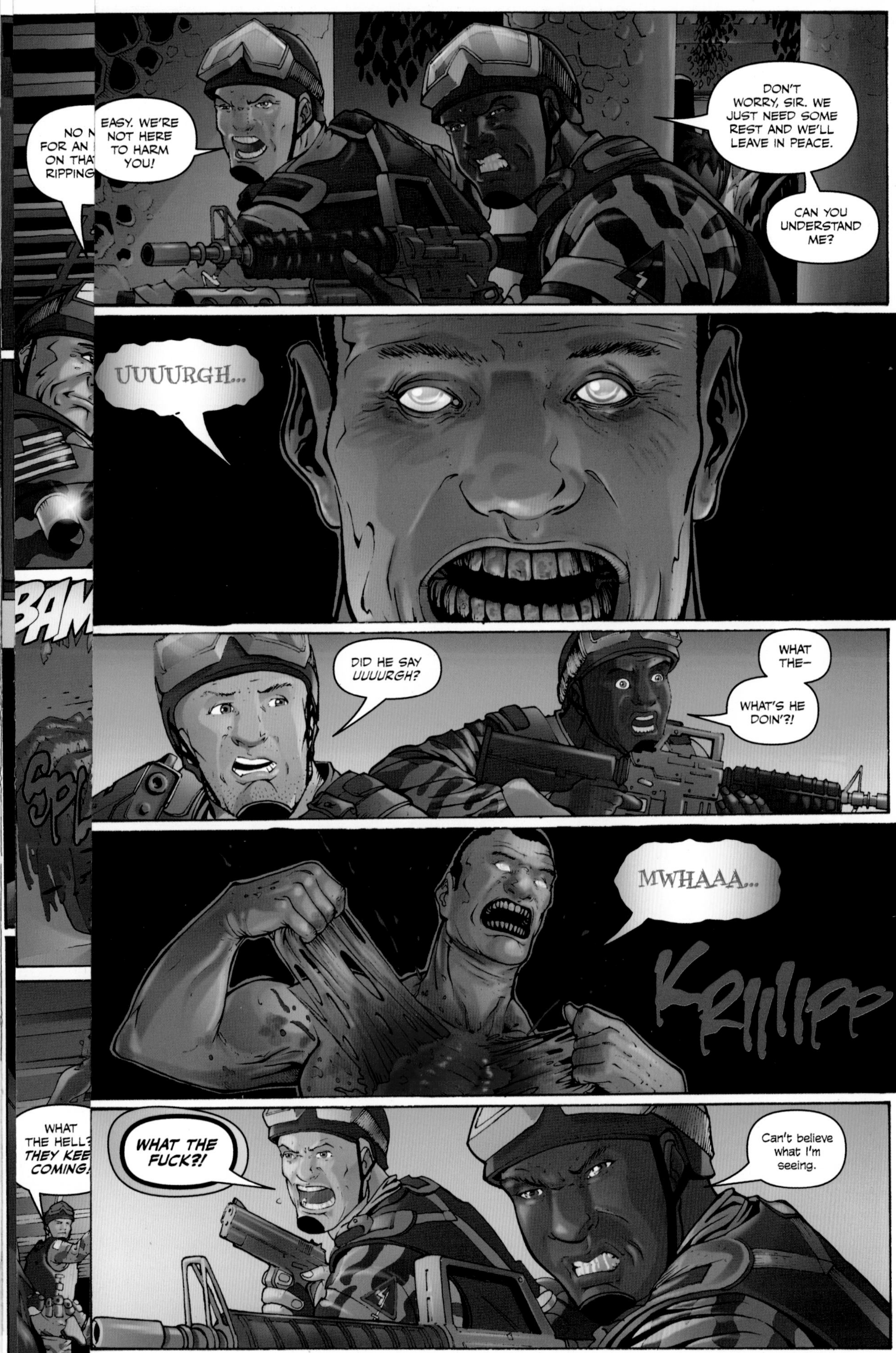
EASY. WE'RE NOT HERE TO HARM YOU!
DON'T WORRY, SIR. WE JUST NEED SOME REST AND WE'LL LEAVE IN PEACE.
CAN YOU UNDERSTAND ME?
UUUURGH...
DID HE SAY *UUUURGH*?
WHAT THE–
WHAT'S HE DOIN'?!
MWHAAA...
KRIIIIPP
WHAT THE FUCK?!
Can't believe what I'm seeing.

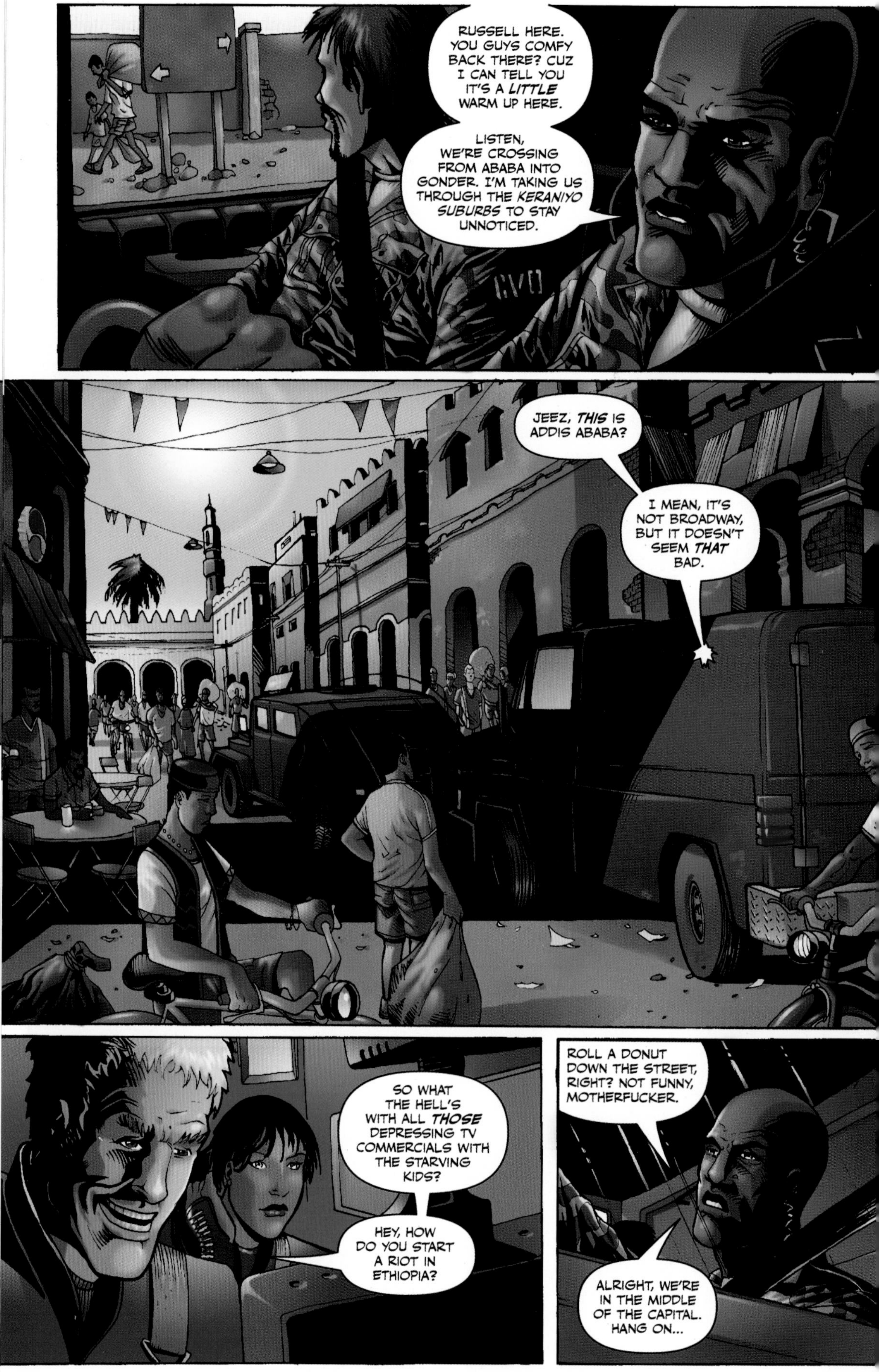
RUSSELL HERE. YOU GUYS COMFY BACK THERE? CUZ I CAN TELL YOU IT'S A *LITTLE* WARM UP HERE.
LISTEN, WE'RE CROSSING FROM ABABA INTO GONDER. I'M TAKING US THROUGH THE *KERANIYO SUBURBS* TO STAY UNNOTICED.
JEEZ, *THIS* IS ADDIS ABABA?
I MEAN, IT'S NOT BROADWAY, BUT IT DOESN'T SEEM *THAT* BAD.
SO WHAT THE HELL'S WITH ALL *THOSE* DEPRESSING TV COMMERCIALS WITH THE STARVING KIDS?
HEY, HOW DO YOU START A RIOT IN ETHIOPIA?
ROLL A DONUT DOWN THE STREET, RIGHT? NOT FUNNY, MOTHERFUCKER.
ALRIGHT, WE'RE IN THE MIDDLE OF THE CAPITAL. HANG ON...

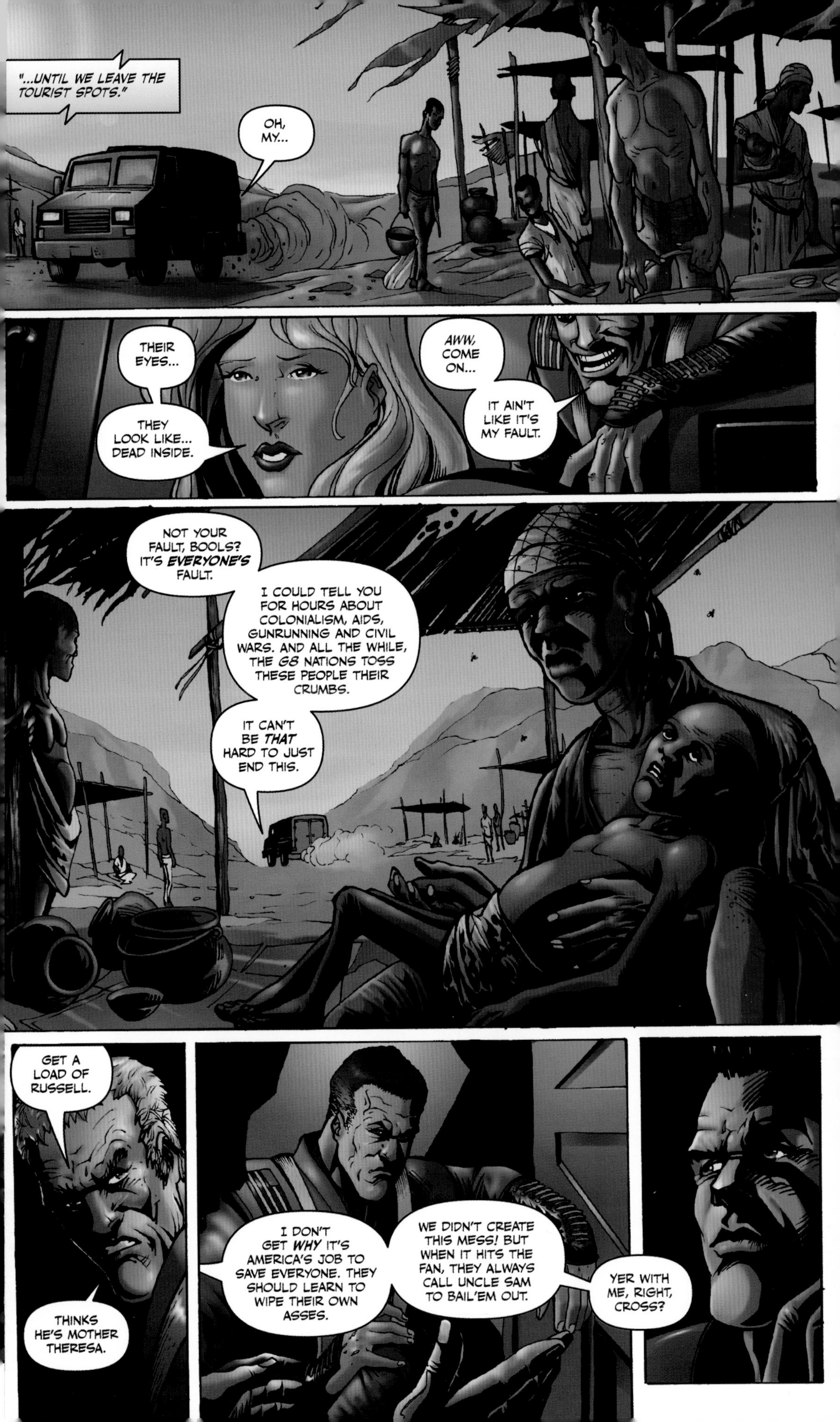
"...UNTIL WE LEAVE THE TOURIST SPOTS."
OH, MY...
THEIR EYES...
THEY LOOK LIKE... DEAD INSIDE.
AWW, COME ON...
IT AIN'T LIKE IT'S MY FAULT.
NOT YOUR FAULT, BOOLS? IT'S EVERYONE'S FAULT.
I COULD TELL YOU FOR HOURS ABOUT COLONIALISM, AIDS, GUNRUNNING AND CIVIL WARS. AND ALL THE WHILE, THE G8 NATIONS TOSS THESE PEOPLE THEIR CRUMBS.
IT CAN'T BE THAT HARD TO JUST END THIS.
GET A LOAD OF RUSSELL.
THINKS HE'S MOTHER THERESA.
I DON'T GET WHY IT'S AMERICA'S JOB TO SAVE EVERYONE. THEY SHOULD LEARN TO WIPE THEIR OWN ASSES.
WE DIDN'T CREATE THIS MESS! BUT WHEN IT HITS THE FAN, THEY ALWAYS CALL UNCLE SAM TO BAIL'EM OUT.
YER WITH ME, RIGHT, CROSS?

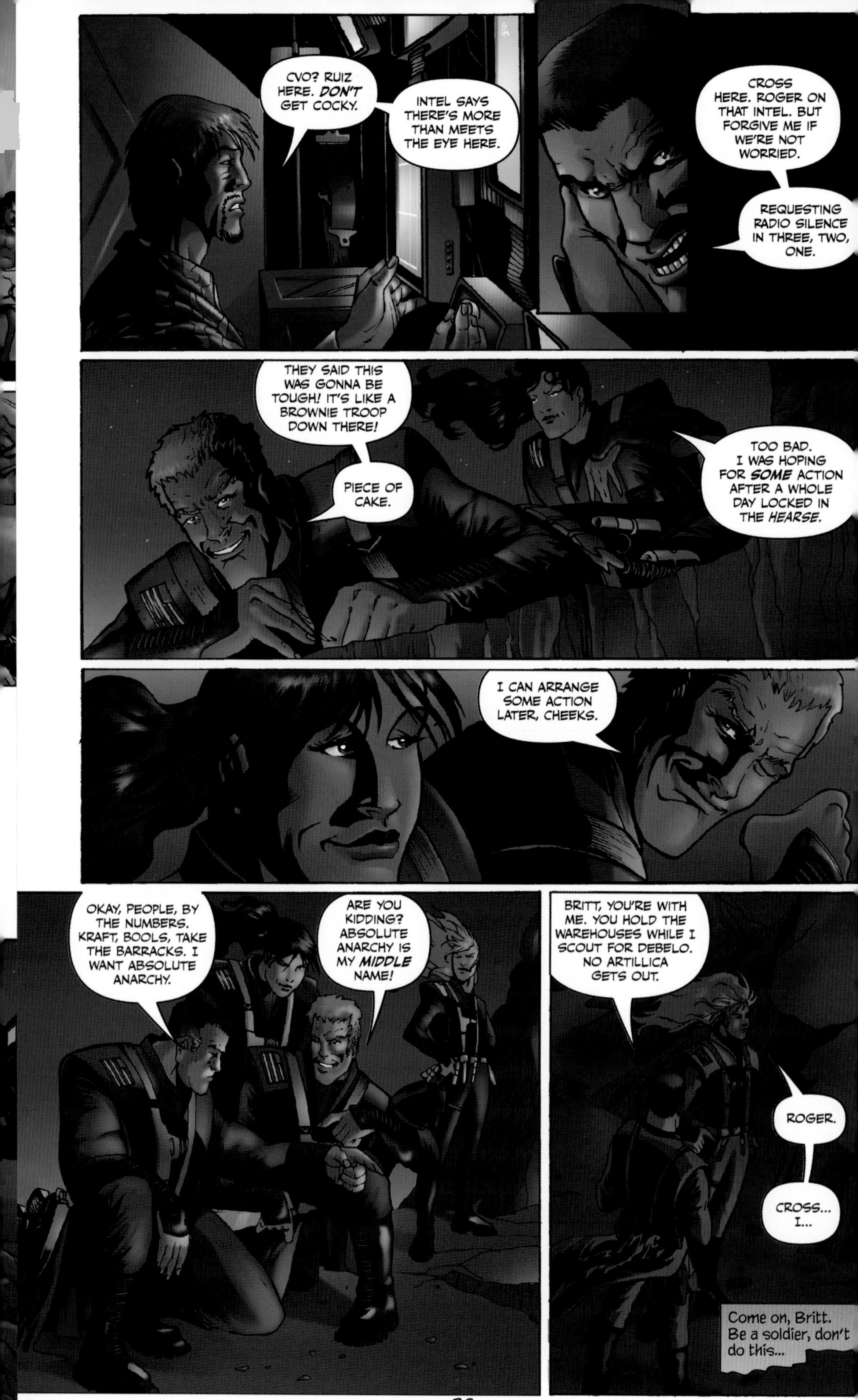
CVO? RUIZ HERE. *DON'T* GET COCKY.
INTEL SAYS THERE'S MORE THAN MEETS THE EYE HERE.
CROSS HERE. ROGER ON THAT INTEL. BUT FORGIVE ME IF WE'RE NOT WORRIED.
REQUESTING RADIO SILENCE IN THREE, TWO, ONE.
THEY SAID THIS WAS GONNA BE TOUGH! IT'S LIKE A BROWNIE TROOP DOWN THERE!
PIECE OF CAKE.
TOO BAD. I WAS HOPING FOR *SOME* ACTION AFTER A WHOLE DAY LOCKED IN THE *HEARSE.*
I CAN ARRANGE SOME ACTION LATER, CHEEKS.
OKAY, PEOPLE, BY THE NUMBERS. KRAFT, BOOLS, TAKE THE BARRACKS. I WANT ABSOLUTE ANARCHY.
ARE YOU KIDDING? ABSOLUTE ANARCHY IS MY *MIDDLE* NAME!
BRITT, YOU'RE WITH ME. YOU HOLD THE WAREHOUSES WHILE I SCOUT FOR DEBELO. NO ARTILLICA GETS OUT.
ROGER.
CROSS... I...
Come on, Britt. Be a soldier, don't do this...

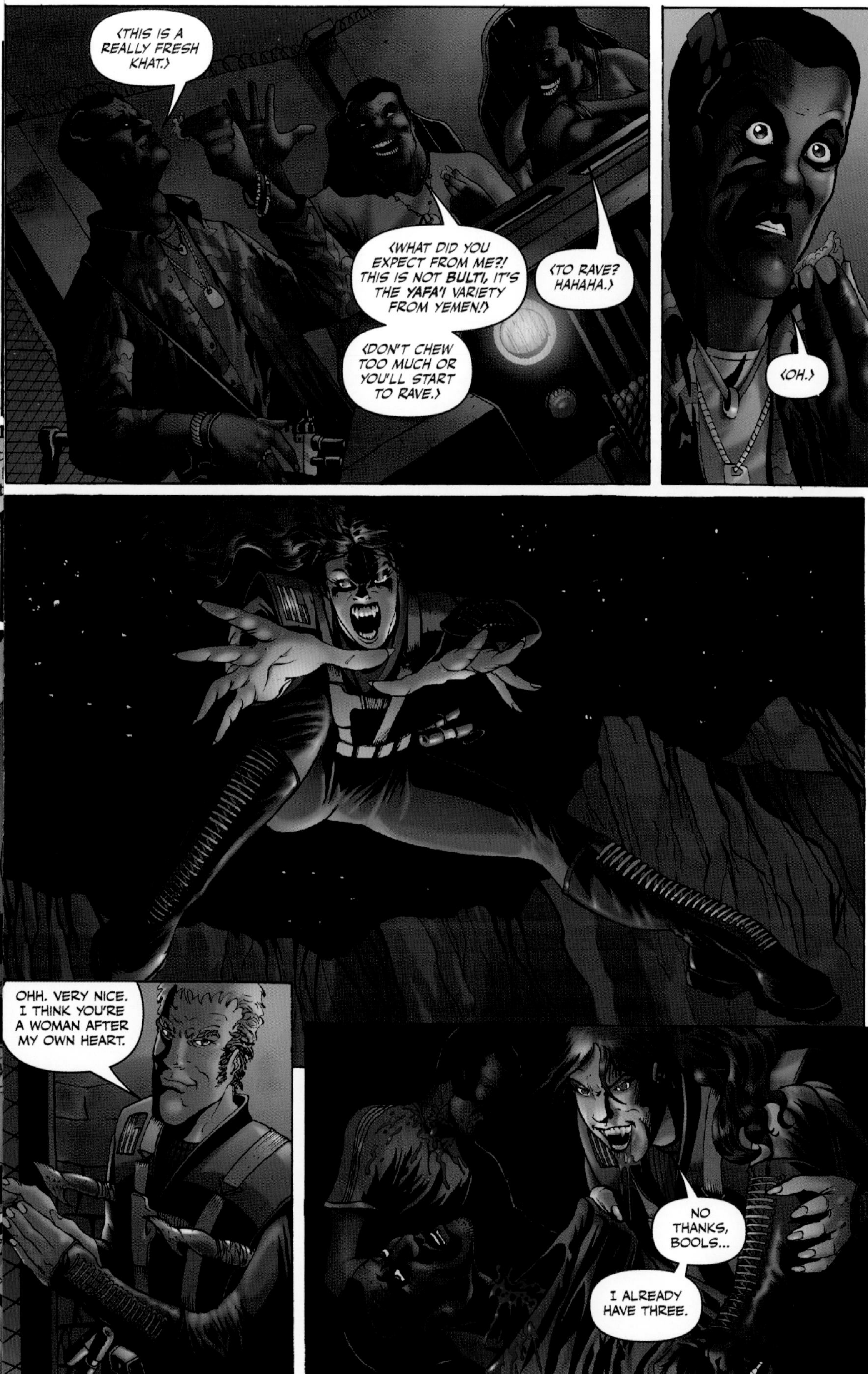
‹THIS IS A REALLY FRESH KHAT.›
‹WHAT DID YOU EXPECT FROM ME?! THIS IS NOT **BULTI**, IT'S THE **YAFA'I** VARIETY FROM YEMEN!›
‹DON'T CHEW TOO MUCH OR YOU'LL START TO RAVE.›
‹TO RAVE? HAHAHA.›
‹OH.›
OHH. VERY NICE. I THINK YOU'RE A WOMAN AFTER MY OWN HEART.
NO THANKS, BOOLS...
I ALREADY HAVE THREE.

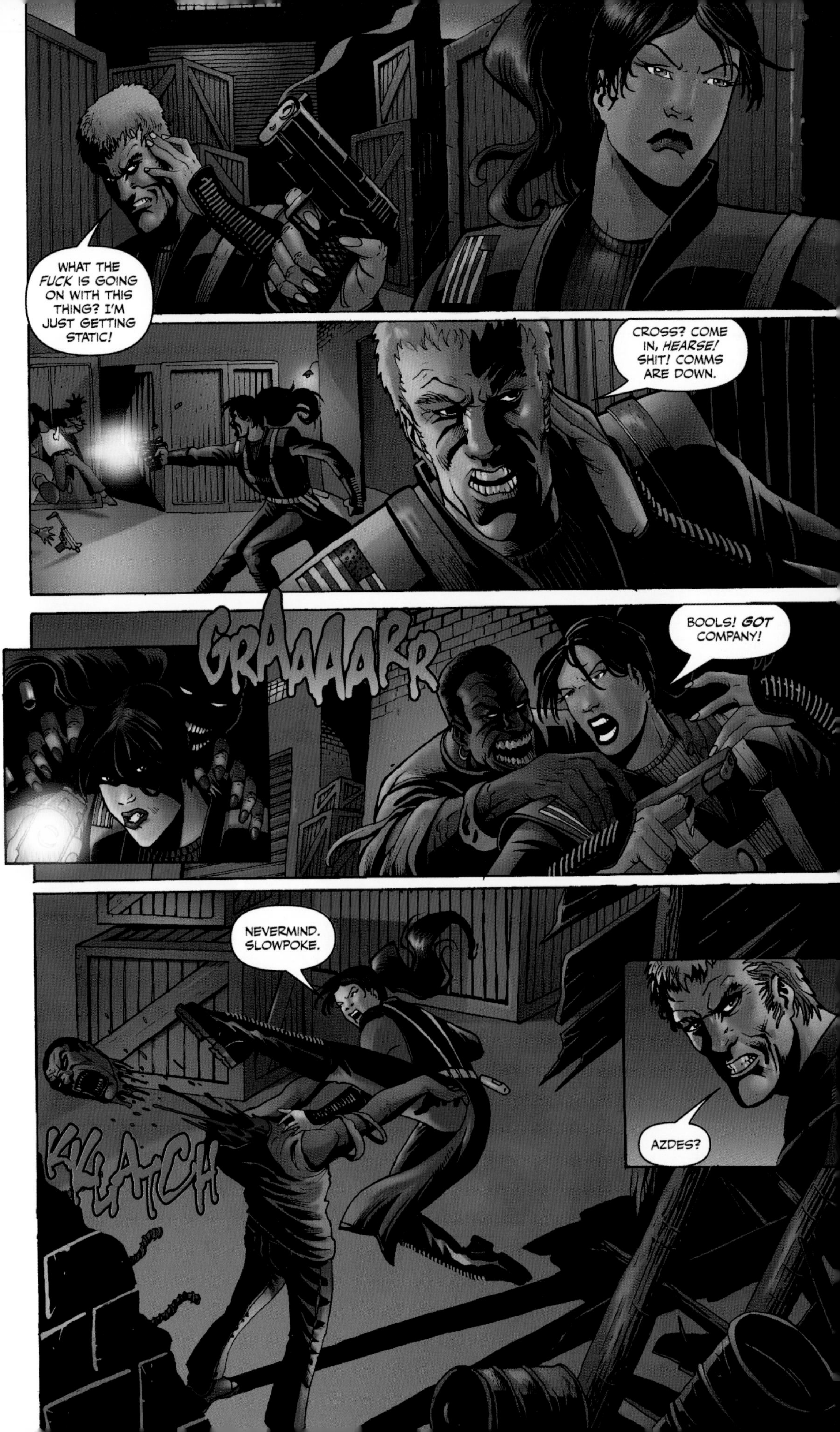
WHAT THE *FUCK* IS GOING ON WITH THIS THING? I'M JUST GETTING STATIC!
CROSS? COME IN, *HEARSE!* SHIT! COMMS ARE DOWN.
GRAAAARR
BOOLS! **GOT** COMPANY!
NEVERMIND. SLOWPOKE.
KLLACH
AZDES?

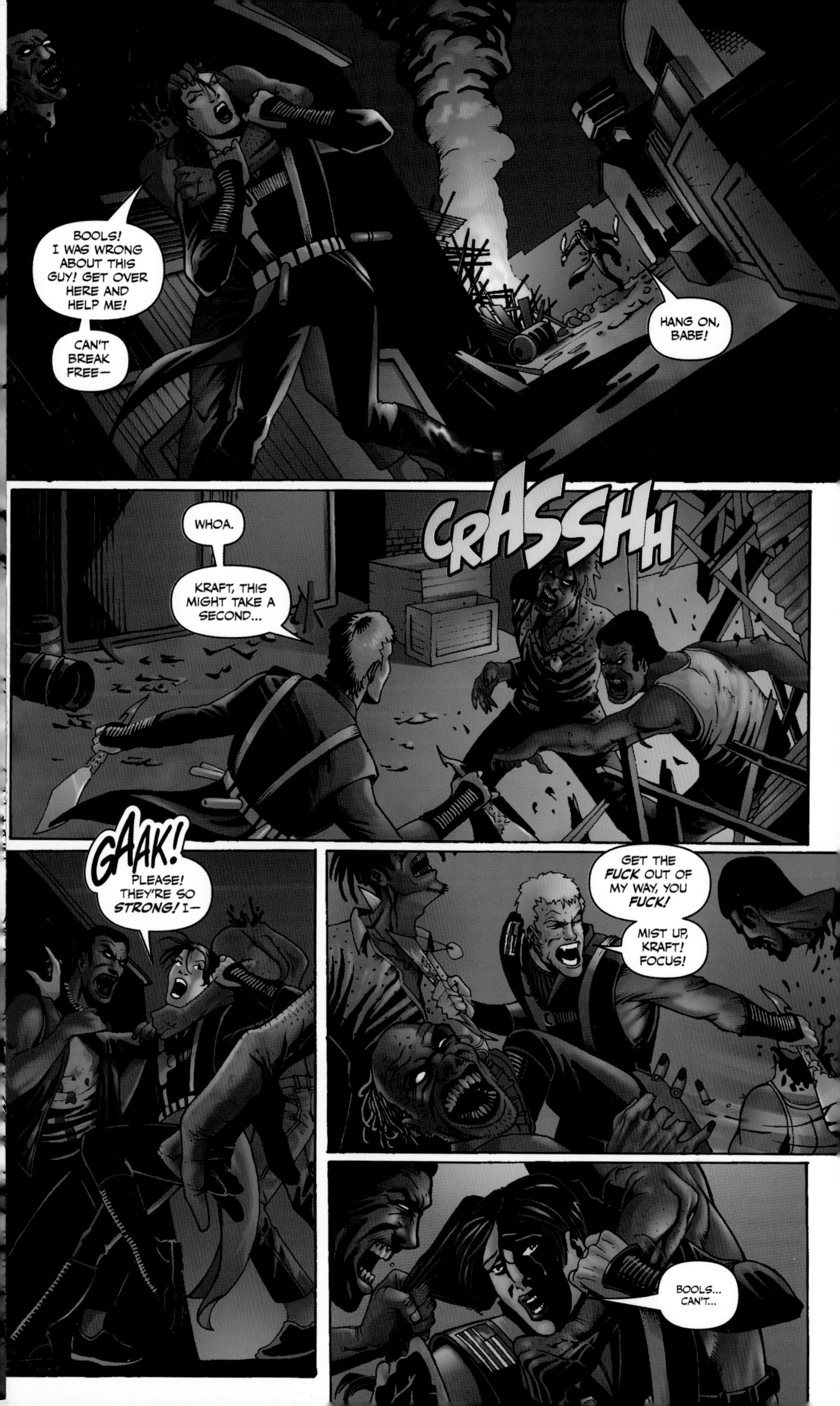
BOOLS! I WAS WRONG ABOUT THIS GUY! GET OVER HERE AND HELP ME!
CAN'T BREAK FREE--
HANG ON, BABE!
CRASSHH
WHOA.
KRAFT, THIS MIGHT TAKE A SECOND...
GAAK!
PLEASE! THEY'RE SO STRONG! I--
GET THE FUCK OUT OF MY WAY, YOU FUCK!
MIST UP, KRAFT! FOCUS!
BOOLS... CAN'T...

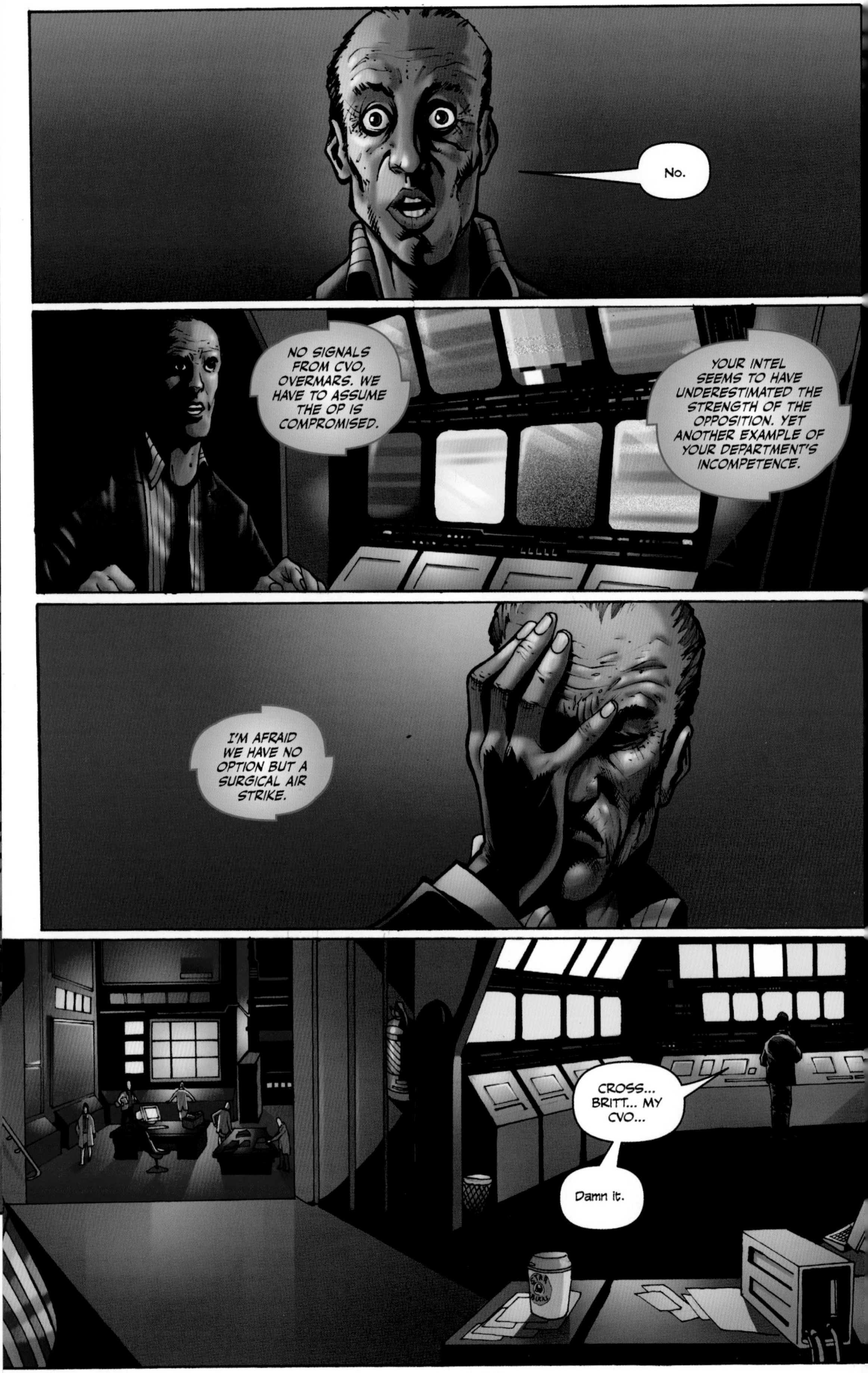
No.
NO SIGNALS FROM CVO, OVERMARS. WE HAVE TO ASSUME THE OP IS COMPROMISED.
YOUR INTEL SEEMS TO HAVE UNDERESTIMATED THE STRENGTH OF THE OPPOSITION. YET ANOTHER EXAMPLE OF YOUR DEPARTMENT'S INCOMPETENCE.
I'M AFRAID WE HAVE NO OPTION BUT A SURGICAL AIR STRIKE.
CROSS... BRITT... MY CVO...
Damn it.

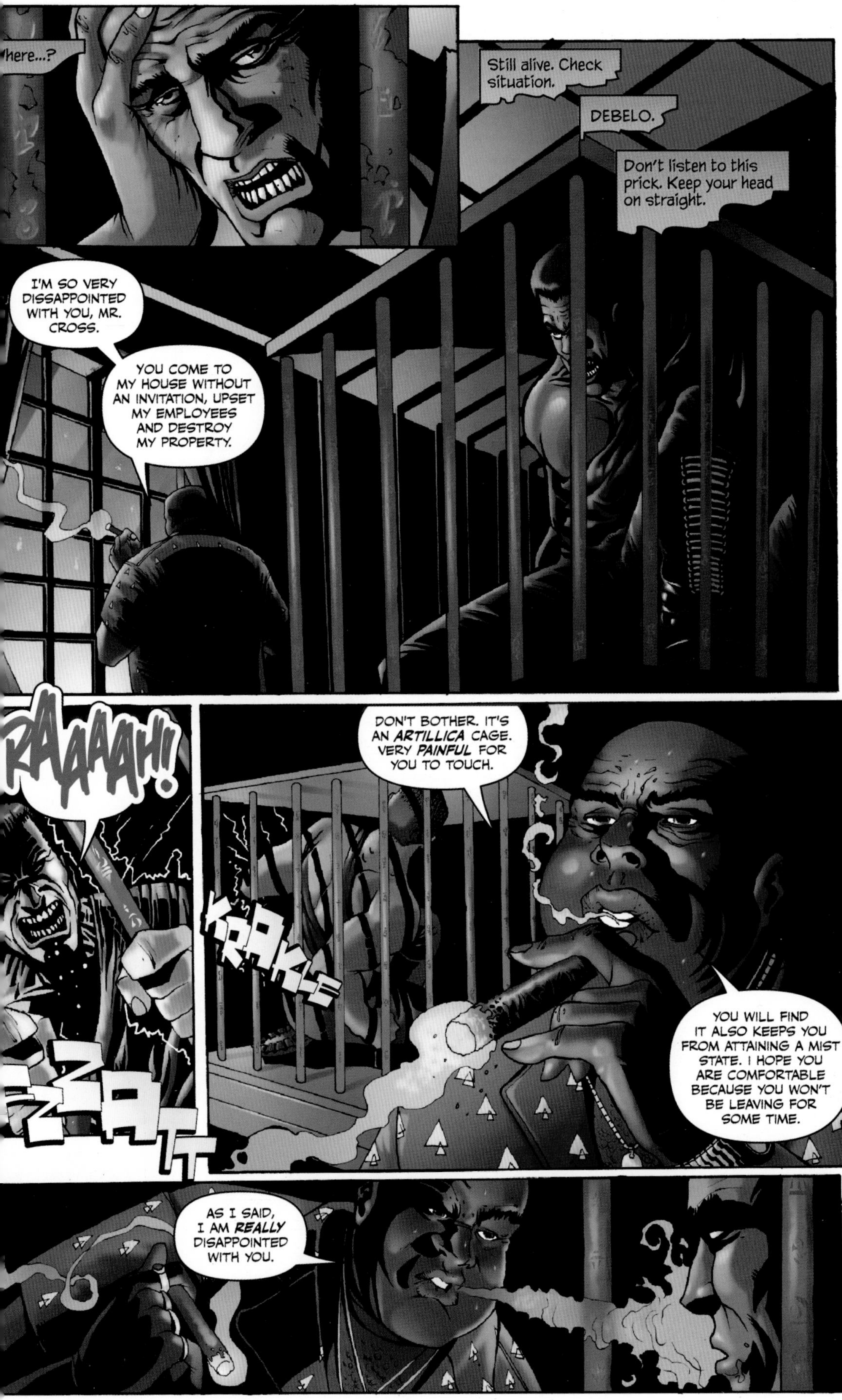
...here...?
Still alive. Check situation.
DEBELO.
Don't listen to this prick. Keep your head on straight.
I'M SO VERY DISSAPPOINTED WITH YOU, MR. CROSS.
YOU COME TO MY HOUSE WITHOUT AN INVITATION, UPSET MY EMPLOYEES AND DESTROY MY PROPERTY.
RAAAAAH!!
ZZATT
KRAKLE
DON'T BOTHER. IT'S AN *ARTILLICA* CAGE. VERY *PAINFUL* FOR YOU TO TOUCH.
YOU WILL FIND IT ALSO KEEPS YOU FROM ATTAINING A MIST STATE. I HOPE YOU ARE COMFORTABLE BECAUSE YOU WON'T BE LEAVING FOR SOME TIME.
AS I SAID, I AM *REALLY* DISAPPOINTED WITH YOU.

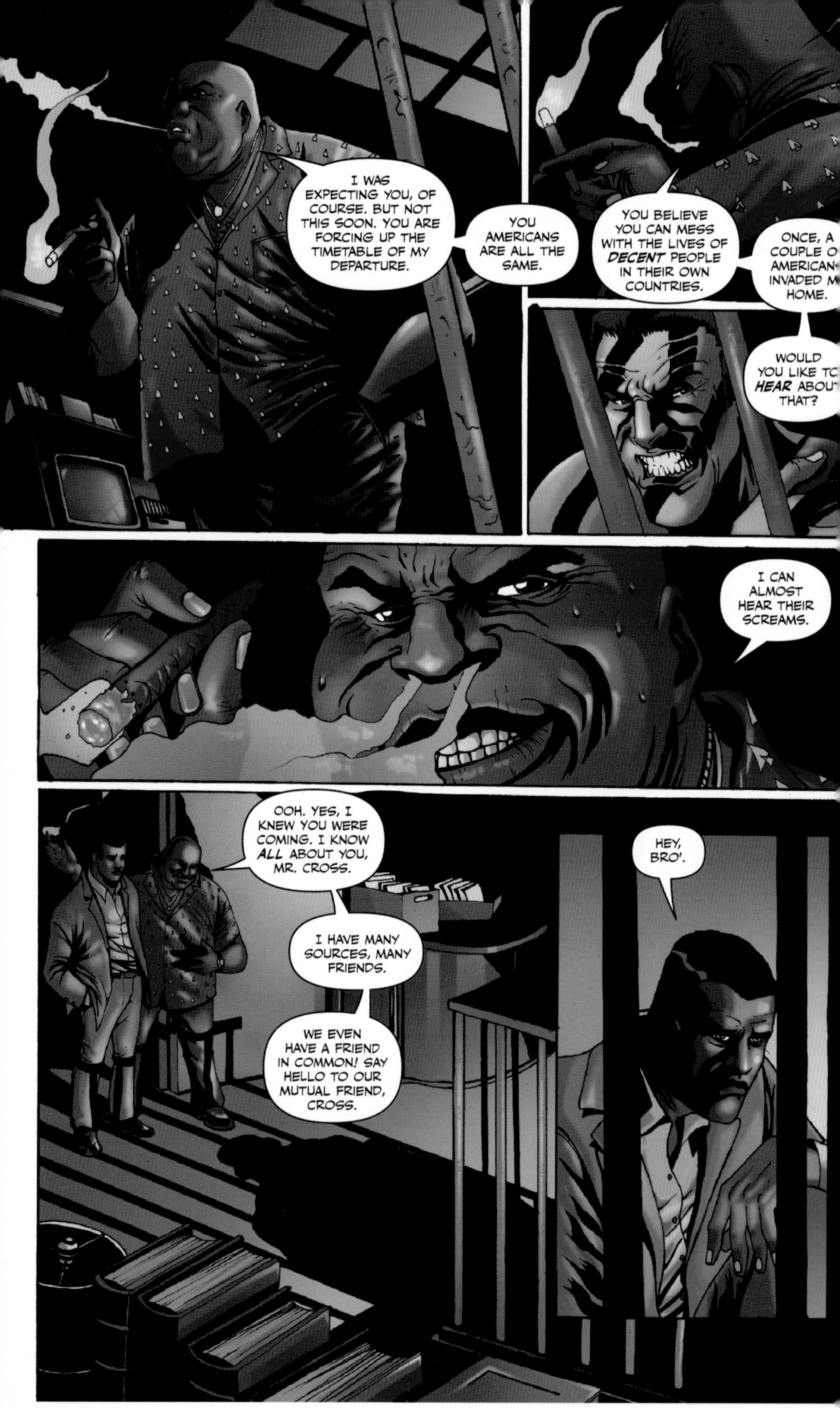
I WAS EXPECTING YOU, OF COURSE. BUT NOT THIS SOON. YOU ARE FORCING UP THE TIMETABLE OF MY DEPARTURE.
YOU AMERICANS ARE ALL THE SAME.
YOU BELIEVE YOU CAN MESS WITH THE LIVES OF DECENT PEOPLE IN THEIR OWN COUNTRIES.
ONCE, A COUPLE O AMERICAN INVADED M HOME.
WOULD YOU LIKE TO HEAR ABOUT THAT?
I CAN ALMOST HEAR THEIR SCREAMS.
OOH. YES, I KNEW YOU WERE COMING. I KNOW ALL ABOUT YOU, MR. CROSS.
I HAVE MANY SOURCES, MANY FRIENDS.
WE EVEN HAVE A FRIEND IN COMMON! SAY HELLO TO OUR MUTUAL FRIEND, CROSS.
HEY, BRO'.

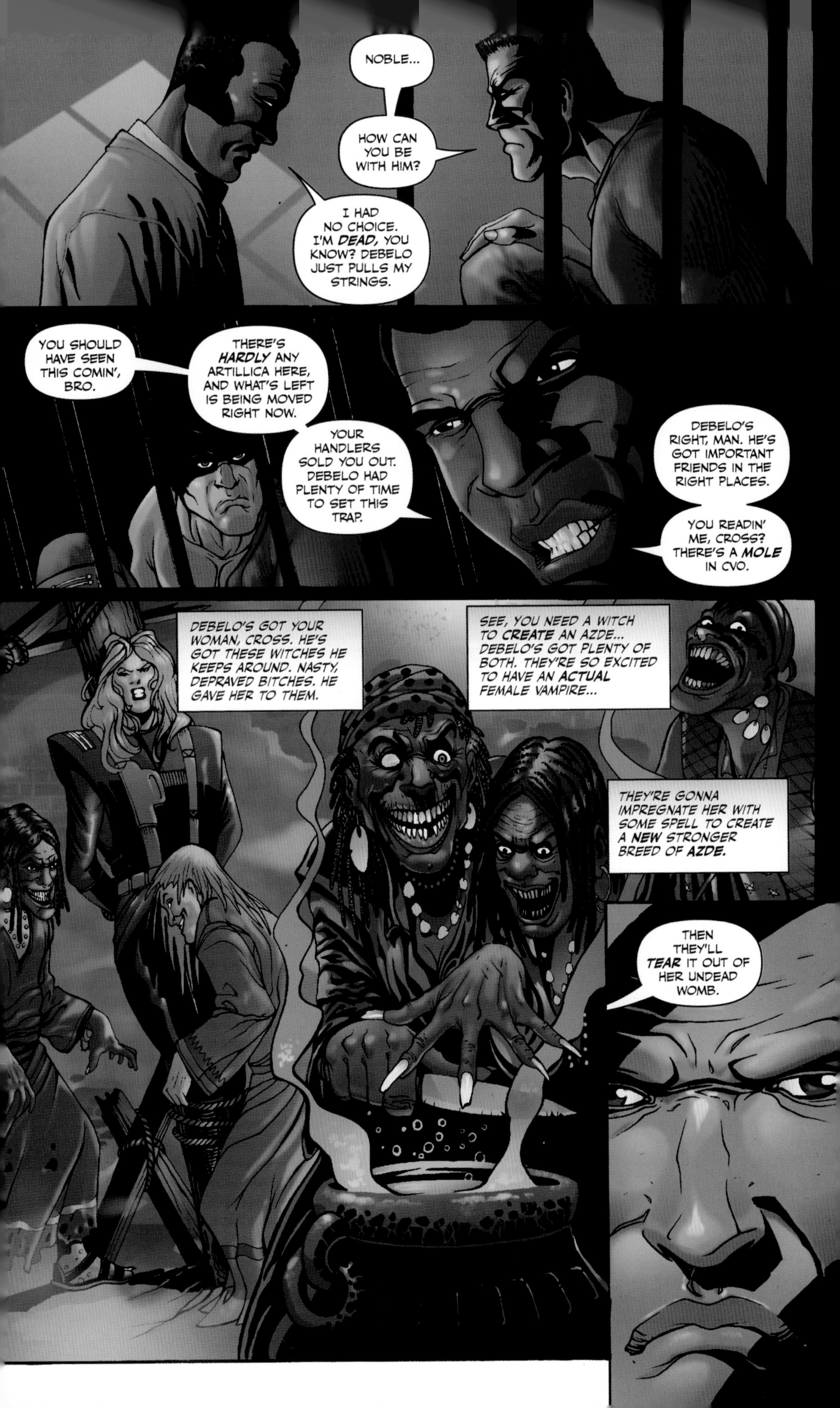
NOBLE...
HOW CAN YOU BE WITH HIM?
I HAD NO CHOICE. I'M DEAD, YOU KNOW? DEBELO JUST PULLS MY STRINGS.
YOU SHOULD HAVE SEEN THIS COMIN', BRO.
THERE'S HARDLY ANY ARTILLICA HERE, AND WHAT'S LEFT IS BEING MOVED RIGHT NOW.
YOUR HANDLERS SOLD YOU OUT. DEBELO HAD PLENTY OF TIME TO SET THIS TRAP.
DEBELO'S RIGHT, MAN. HE'S GOT IMPORTANT FRIENDS IN THE RIGHT PLACES.
YOU READIN' ME, CROSS? THERE'S A MOLE IN CVO.
DEBELO'S GOT YOUR WOMAN, CROSS. HE'S GOT THESE WITCHES HE KEEPS AROUND. NASTY, DEPRAVED BITCHES. HE GAVE HER TO THEM.
SEE, YOU NEED A WITCH TO CREATE AN AZDE... DEBELO'S GOT PLENTY OF BOTH. THEY'RE SO EXCITED TO HAVE AN ACTUAL FEMALE VAMPIRE...
THEY'RE GONNA IMPREGNATE HER WITH SOME SPELL TO CREATE A NEW STRONGER BREED OF AZDE.
THEN THEY'LL TEAR IT OUT OF HER UNDEAD WOMB.

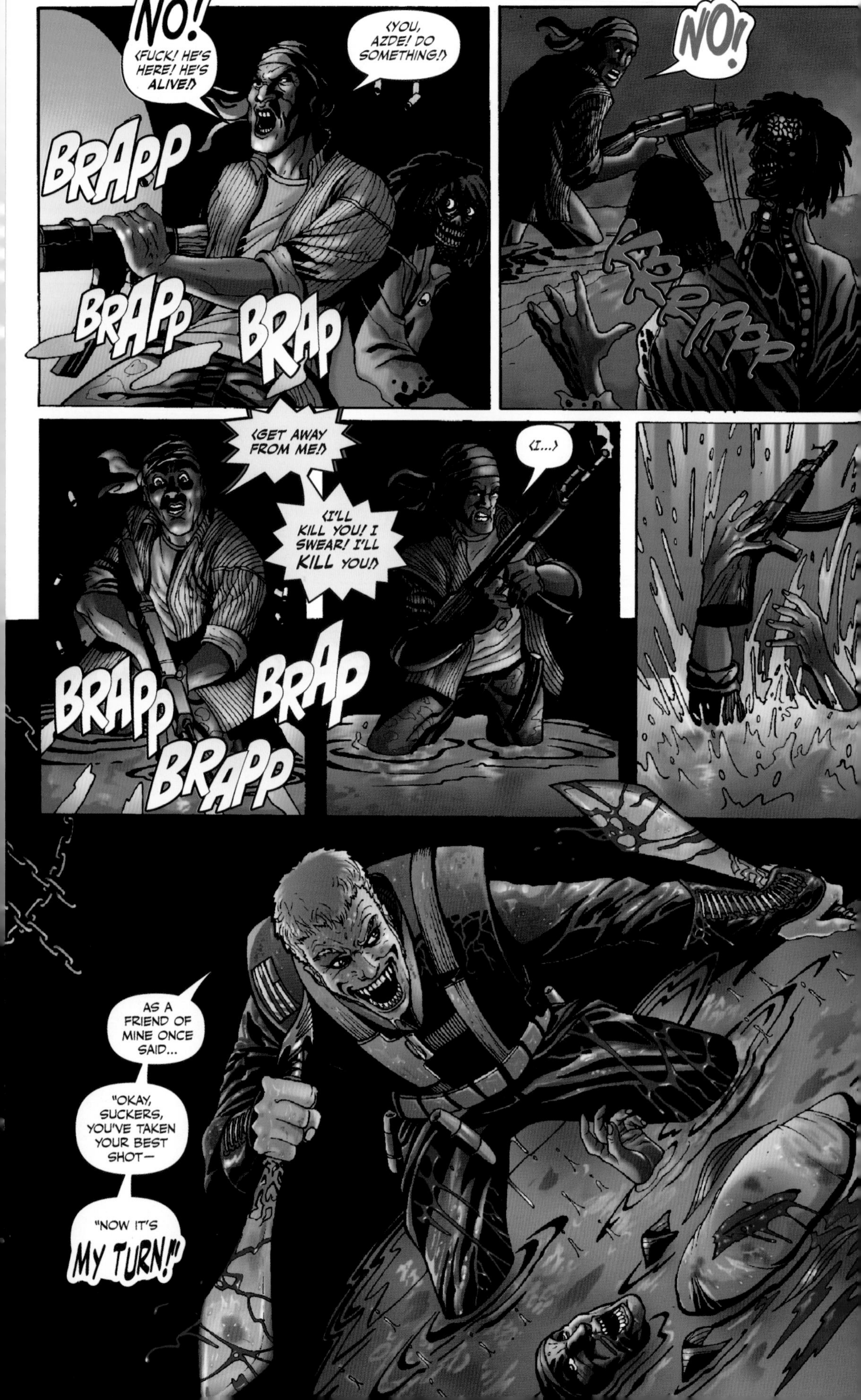
NO!
‹FUCK! HE'S HERE! HE'S ALIVE!›
‹YOU, AZDE! DO SOMETHING!›
BRAPP
BRAPP
BRAP
NO!
KRRIPPP
‹GET AWAY FROM ME!›
‹I'LL KILL YOU! I SWEAR! I'LL KILL YOU!›
‹I...›
BRAPP
BRAP
BRAPP
AS A FRIEND OF MINE ONCE SAID...
"OKAY, SUCKERS, YOU'VE TAKEN YOUR BEST SHOT—
"NOW IT'S MY TURN!"

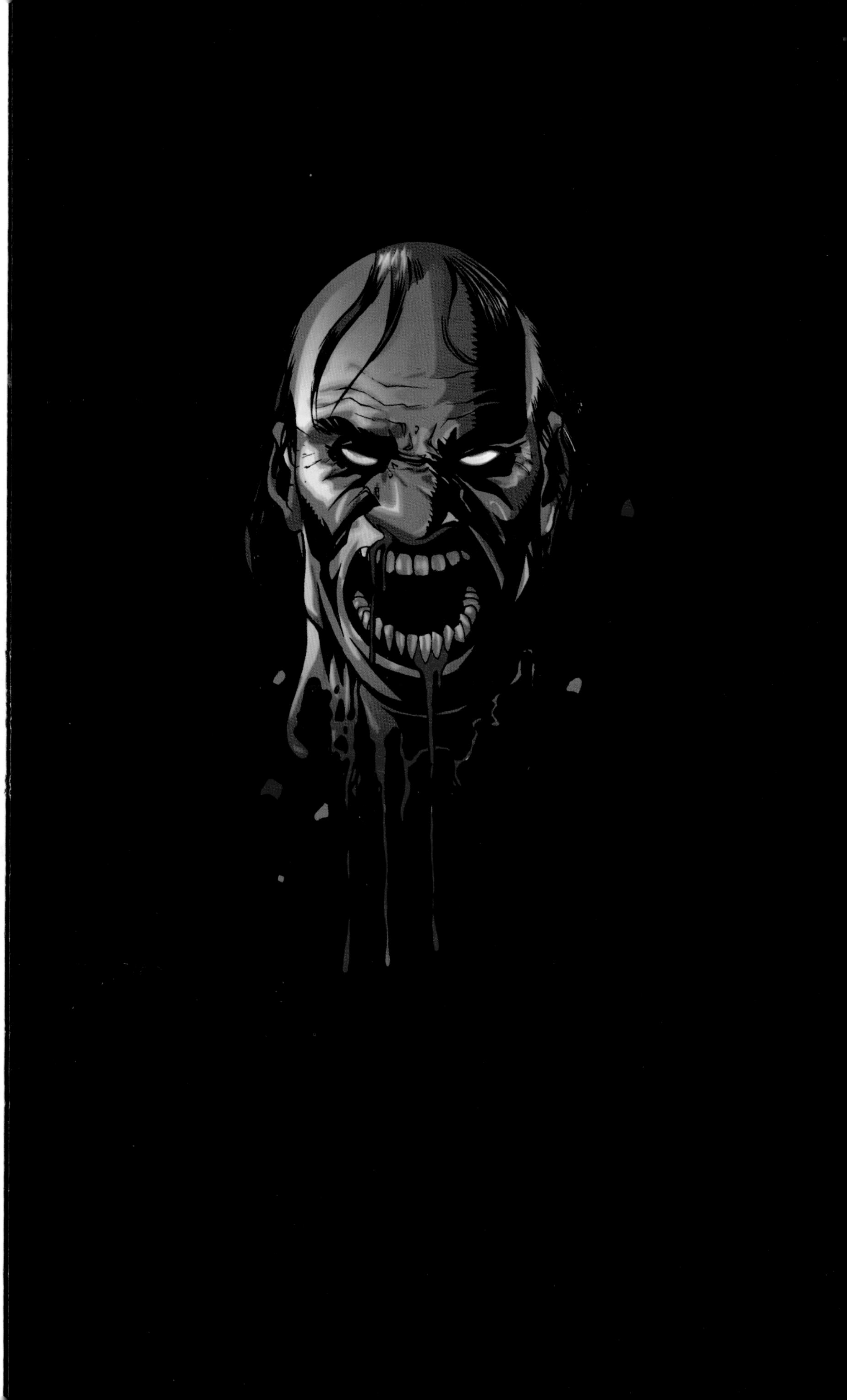

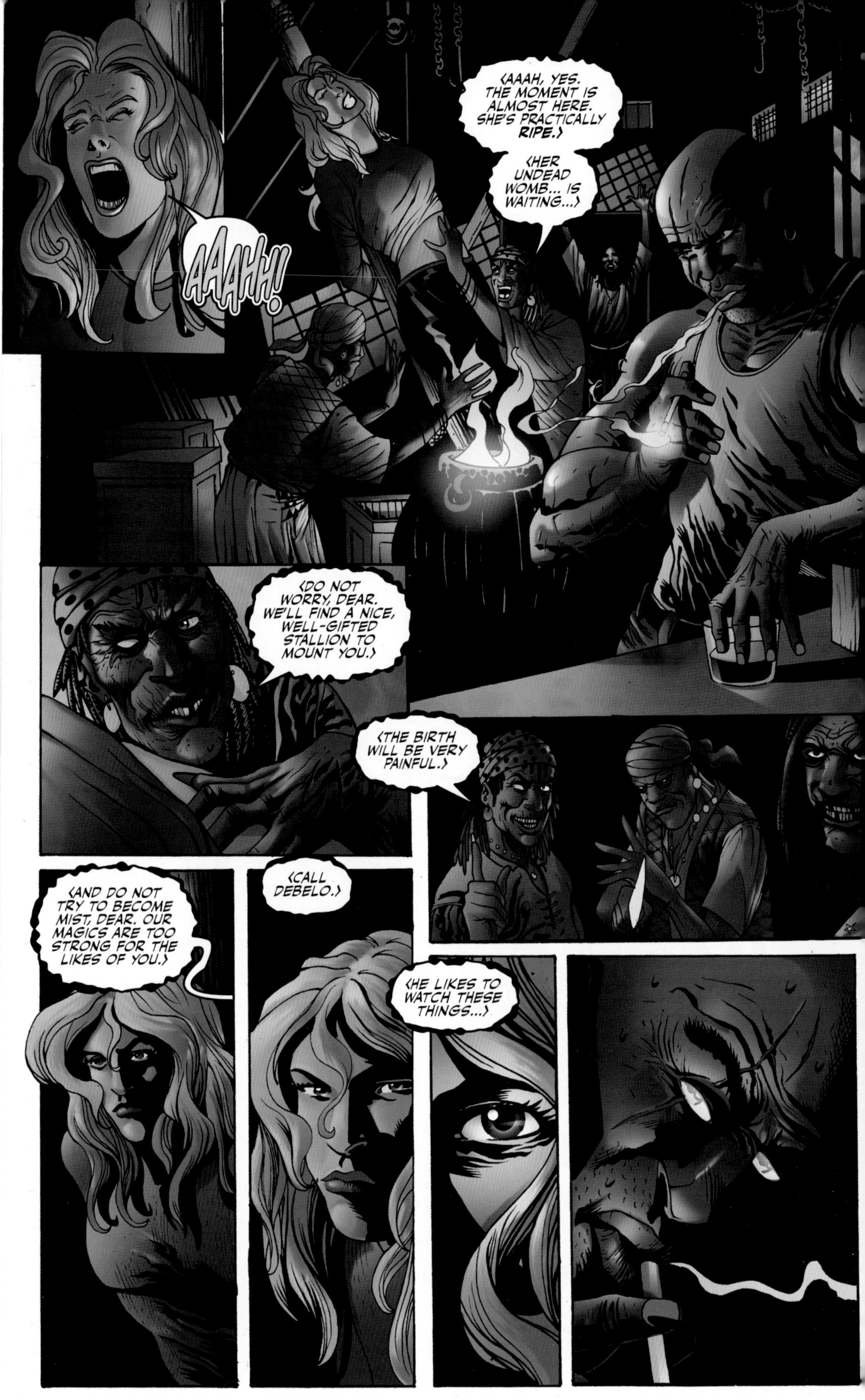

AAAHH!
‹AAAH, YES. THE MOMENT IS ALMOST HERE. SHE'S PRACTICALLY **RIPE**.›
‹HER UNDEAD WOMB... IS WAITING...›
‹DO NOT WORRY, DEAR. WE'LL FIND A NICE, WELL-GIFTED STALLION TO MOUNT YOU.›
‹THE BIRTH WILL BE VERY PAINFUL.›
‹AND DO NOT TRY TO BECOME MIST, DEAR. OUR MAGICS ARE TOO STRONG FOR THE LIKES OF YOU.›
‹CALL DEBELO.›
‹HE LIKES TO WATCH THESE THINGS...›

ARGH!!
BASTARD!

"YOU KNO[...]
TELETRAN[...]
ARTILLIC[...]"

"IT[...]
TO[...]
OR[...]"

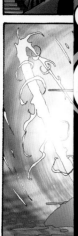

‹...EVEN WHEN HE'S NOT PART OF IT.›

‹HEE, HEE! IT REMINDS ME OF MY YOUTH...›

CLICK

‹YOU, WHAT DO Y--?›

BRAPP

BRAPP

EEEK!!

GOOD PET.

VERY GOOD PET.

NOW, IF YOU'D BE A LOVE AND *UNTIE* ME...

YES, YOU'RE A GOOD BOY. THAT DAMNED MAGIC HAS LEFT ME ALL *DROOPSY*...

NOW, IF YOU'D JUST *INVITE* THIS GIRL TO DINNER...

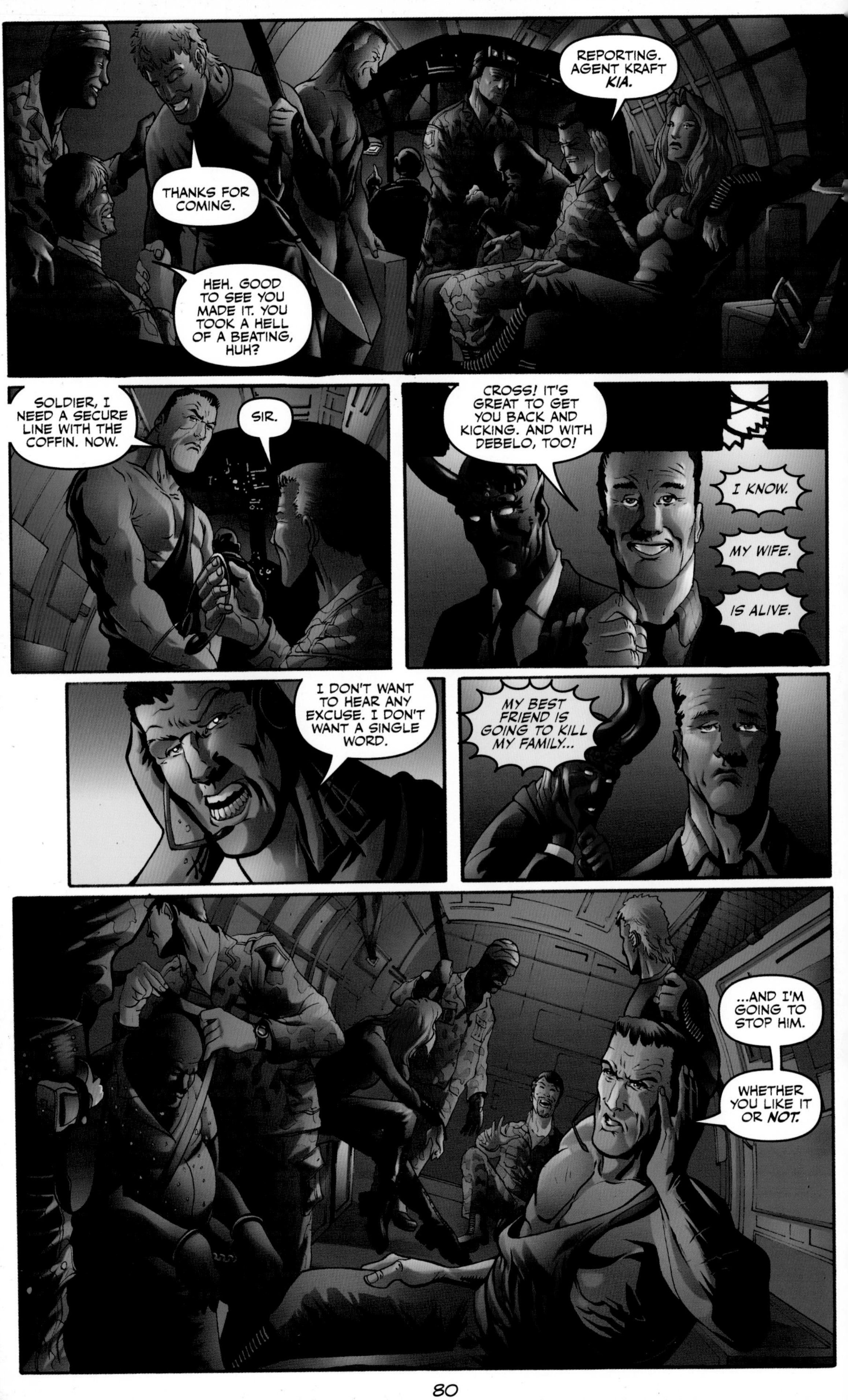
REPORTING. AGENT KRAFT KIA.
THANKS FOR COMING.
HEH. GOOD TO SEE YOU MADE IT. YOU TOOK A HELL OF A BEATING, HUH?
SOLDIER, I NEED A SECURE LINE WITH THE COFFIN. NOW.
SIR.
CROSS! IT'S GREAT TO GET YOU BACK AND KICKING. AND WITH DEBELO, TOO!
I KNOW.
MY WIFE.
IS ALIVE.
I DON'T WANT TO HEAR ANY EXCUSE. I DON'T WANT A SINGLE WORD.
MY BEST FRIEND IS GOING TO KILL MY FAMILY...
...AND I'M GOING TO STOP HIM.
WHETHER YOU LIKE IT OR NOT.

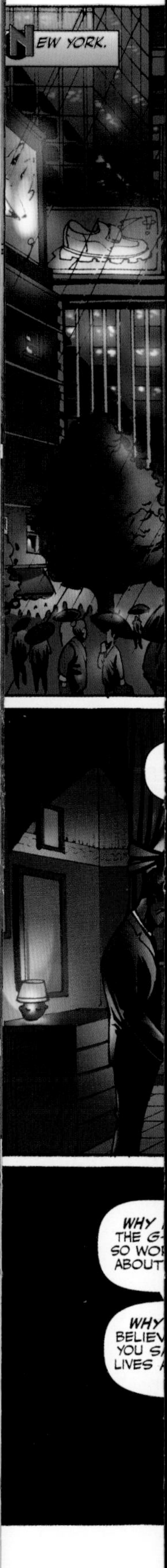
NEW YORK.
WHY
THE G-
SO WOR
ABOUT
WHY
BELIEV
YOU S
LIVES
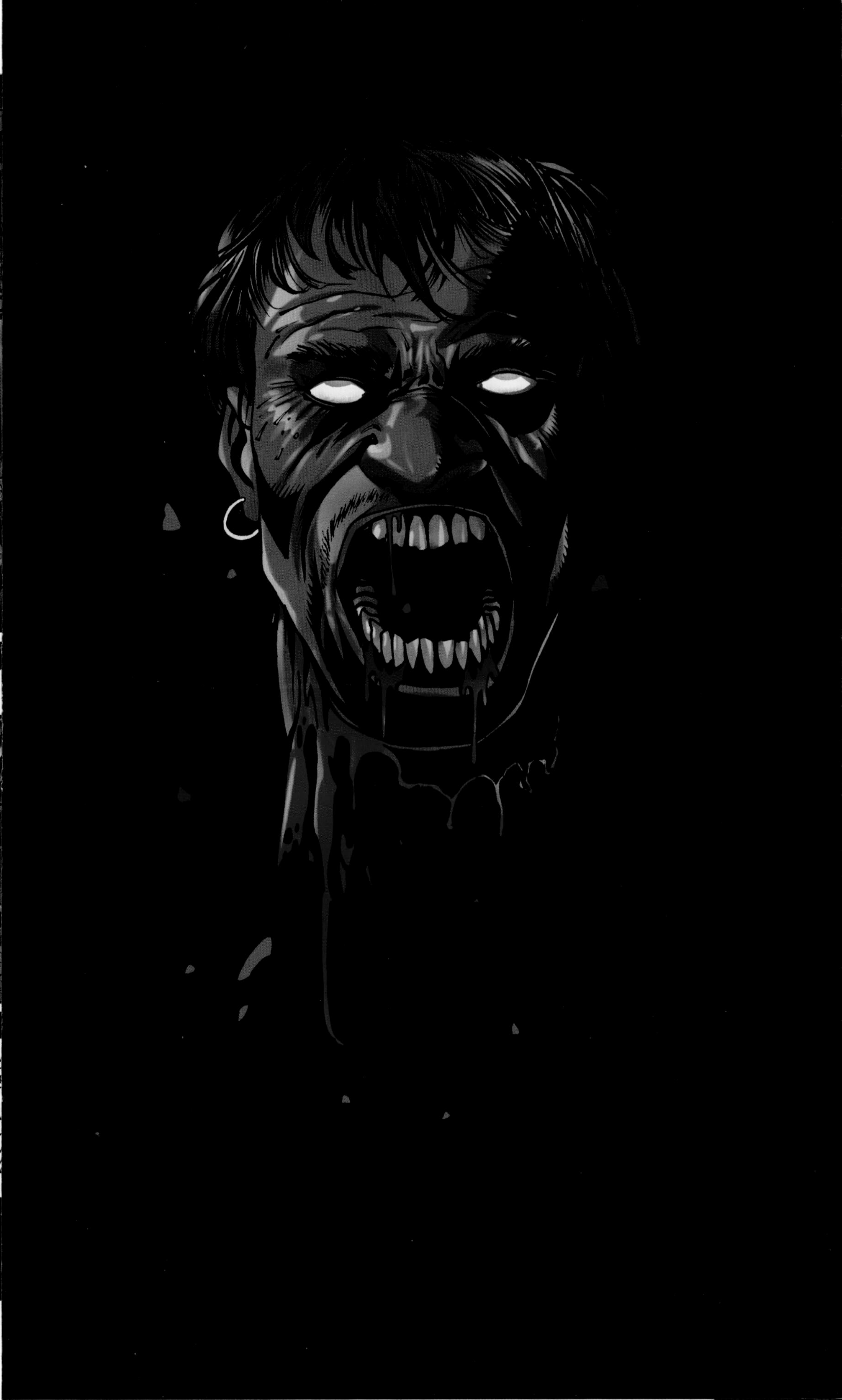

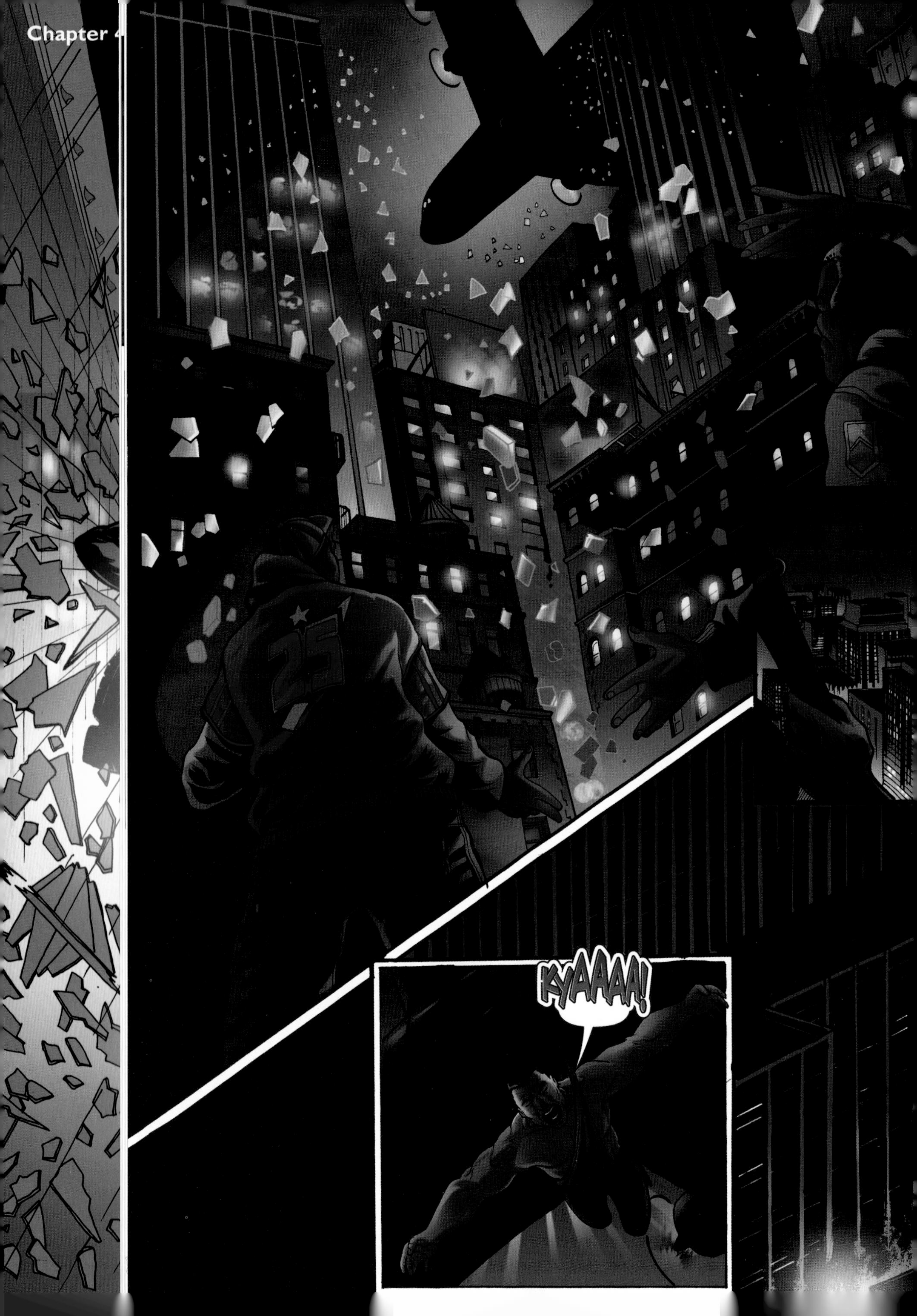
KYAAAA!